INTRODUCTION

There are many famous people who ... or who spent part of their working life i ... e have been world famous, others have ... ...gures and all have contributed in a number of different ways to Kirkcaldy's Heritage.

When the new Town House was opened in Kirkcaldy phase one in 1953 and phase two in 1956, there was a board in place inside the front door with the names of six of 'Kirkcaldy's Famous Sons'. Now there are eight.

It is not known on whose advice these were chosen nor why there were no daughters included. By studying the list many may wonder what these six contributed and what their connection was with Kirkcaldy, other than being born here.

The six famous sons are:- Robert Adam, Adam Smith, Bailie Robert Philp, Dr John Philip, Sir Sandford Fleming and John McDouall Stuart. With the exception of Robert Philp all these men are well known international figures with contributions made to the world at large. Many people may never have heard of some of the names nor be aware of where in Kirkcaldy links can still be seen to remind us that they once lived here.

The Society is producing three books, the first two cover those who have made contributions mainly outwith industry while the third book will cover the industrialists who have given jobs to the people of Kirkcaldy and who have also given much in the way of various benefits to this town, men like Michael Nairn and Michael Beveridge.

The bulk of the names are those of men because in the past the women had little opportunity to develop their own talents in the professions or in industry, but they are behind every great man either as a mother, a wife or both.

This book covers William Adam and his son Robert, Bailie Robert Philp and his distant cousin Dr John Philip, Marjory Fleming and Sir Sandford Fleming (not related). Only three are on the original list of "Kirkcaldy's Famous Sons" in the Town House.

Bust of William Adam on his grave at Greyfriars Church

Duff House, Banffshire designed by William Adam

WILLIAM ADAM 1689-1748 (59 years)

William Adam's links with Kirkcaldy stem from the fact that he was born and brought up in the Linktown of Abbotshall, now part of Kirkcaldy and later had many business interests in the town.

He married Mary Robertson from Linktown and lived in Gladney House which he had built earlier for his partner who later became also his father-in-law.

William Adam was the only child of John Adam and Helen Cranstoun. John Adam was the second son of Archibald Adam of Queensmanor near Forfar, but he came to work in Linktown setting up a mason's business.

Helen Cranstoun was the daughter of Lord Cranstoun who was a soldier, but the troubles of the 17th century involved him in a duel in which he killed his opponent. He was forced to flee to the Continent where he became a soldier of fortune with Gustavus Adolphus.

William was born in 1689 and was baptised on October 24th 1689, probably in Abbotshall Church. Little is known about his education and childhood but he probably attended the local school, which would have been in the Linktown of Abbotshall. He was apprenticed as a mason and went to work with his father. In 1707 the Act of Union of the Parliaments between Scotland and England was passed when William was 18.

William's father John Adam had come from farming stock but had decided that this was not the life for him, thus he established himself as a mason in Linktown. (This was created a Parish in 1650). At this time masons were considered to be "architects" and builders. Architects at that time were considered to be skilled tradesmen, but he obviously trained his only son in the art of design and building as William followed very successfully in his father's footsteps. John Adam, William's father is known to have been paid for some work done on Raith House which was built in 1694.

Blairadam House 2000, with Keith Adam.

General Wade's Bridge, Aberfeldy. Designed by William Adam.

Sir William Bruce of Kinross House, the Royal Architect, was commissioned to build Hopetoun House, by Charles Hope later the first Earl of Hopetoun. Work was started in 1699 and the main work completed in 1707. Sir William Bruce of Balcaskie and Kinross, a well-known architect/designer, had built Kinross House to replace the older "New House of Loch Leven", after he had bought the Estate in 1675, from William Douglas 8th Earl of Morton. The house started in 1680, was completed in 1693. He was a Jacobite and Episcopalian, who was locked up and imprisoned. He was in and out of prison between 1693 and 1707 and was finally released in 1708. Sir William Bruce died in 1710 and is buried in the family mausoleum, on the banks of Loch Leven, near Kinross House.

In 1721 the wings of Hopetoun House were added, designed by William Adam and later the front entrance with a portico and curved stairs. This was later redesigned, the front portico and stairs being removed to give a recessed entrance with a broad central staircase, fanning out at the base. (1750-51) As William died in 1748, three of his sons John, Robert and James finished the work and embarked on the redesigned front.

However William Adam's Grand Tour was not to be in Italy but he did travel extensively. His travels covered the Low Countries and London where he picked up many ideas to brighten up Scottish architecture. William Adam was a very successful architect and in great demand in many places in Scotland and elsewhere in England from 1720 when he had no less than half a dozen houses under construction in addition to Gladney House which was completed in 1711.

In 1714 William Adam went into partnership with William Robertson, in Linktown, to make Dutch-type pantiles, amongst many items. Pantiles were rapidly becoming popular for roofing instead of thatch. They established the Linktown Brick and Tile Works, leasing the rich local clay beds later known as Adamsfield, from Andrew Ramsay, the Superior.

Hopetoun House

William Adam's Grave, Greyfriars

William Robertson had been Baron Bailie to the Countess of Wemyss and Cromartie in Gladney, a small cotton-spinning hamlet near Ceres. In 1687 he became "Laird of Gladney". When the Countess died in 1705 Robertson became tacksman with coal rights in Abbotshall, feued from Andrew Ramsay. Hence the Robertsons moved to the Linktown of Abbotshall, a Burgh of Barony adjacent to Kirkcaldy, a Royal Burgh.

In 1716 when William Adam was 27 he married Mary Robertson the 17 year old (1699-1761) daughter of William Robertson. She was the sister of the Reverend William Robertson of Gladney, who at that time was minister at Greyfriars Church in Edinburgh; William moved into Gladney House which he shared with William Robertson. The partnership between the two Williams continued until William Robertson died in 1728.

William Adam was very successful in his career as an architect. He also had interests in many commercial ventures among them "Barley Mills, Timber Mills, Coal Works, Salt Pans, Highways and Farms". William Adam also had coal works and salt pans in Cockenzie and Pinkie on the south side of the Forth. In 1711 he pioneered a Dutch-type barley mill in West Saltoun.(East Lothian)

William Adam later outgrew the town of Kirkcaldy/Linktown and spread his wings over Scotland and later moved his residence to the Canongate, Edinburgh and his country estate to Blairadam, Fife. He travelled extensively up and down the country, sometimes by coach but more often on horseback as it was quicker.

In 1729 William was made "Surveyor to the King's Works in Scotland". After the 1745 Uprising much work was created in building the Highland Forts, Fort Augustus, Fort William and notably Fort George, in order to control the Highlanders. Work on Fort George started in 1748 and finished in 1760. As William died in June 1748, most of that work was continued by his sons John, Robert and James. William was also the designer of General Wade's famous bridge at Aberfeldy and some of Wade's Highland roads. William Adam was responsib1e for building Newliston House, at Kirkliston, now for sale, also Mavisbank 1722-27, now in a ruinous state. (1995) Some of the

William Adam Scottish houses open to the public are:- House of Dun, Duff House, Floors Castle, Haddo House, Mellerstain and Hopetoun House.

William Adam bought Blairadam Estate from Sir John Bruce Hope, grandson of Sir William Bruce of Kinross House in 1731. It was then called Blair Crambeth and soon was shortened to The Blair and later Blair Adam. The land was at this time merely bleak moorland, a part of Kinross Estate. Later he developed the land, enlarging the area to 3000 acres and built Blairadam House close by a place he called Maryburgh, named after his wife, Mary. When William bought the land it was bare with but a single ash tree. He planted many trees when he developed the land and built the house. The house has remained in Adam hands, over 250 years ever since it was built except for a brief two year period.

Blairadam is not a grand house like so many of the William and Robert Adam houses. The reason for this was that there were grand schemes for other people's houses but there was never enough cash to carry out the intended plans as Robert's brother John always seemed to be having to bale his brothers out of some financial difficulty.

Over the years William Adam built up the Estate, building the house. It was his son John who developed the gardens after inheriting the Estate after his father died in 1748, having acquired an interest in landscaping gardens. It was John who continued the development of the gardens in typical Adam style, planting many trees including the famous walled arboretum, where the monument tells of William's start and John's further work. The listed monument was built by John's son William.

William Adam must have been wealthy in his time as he had many business investments, a public office from 1729 and various private architectural contracts such as Hopetoun House.

One of his unfortunate ventures was the building of Duff House, Banff for Lord Braco when he assumed he had a free financial hand. Lord Braco was furious at the expense which he claimed he had not sanctioned and took William to court. The case was finally won by William Adam shortly before he died and the money due to him was paid. Duff House was probably his finest work.

There were 10 living children of his marriage with Mary (13 in total) and it was a very happy family. However only three of the siblings ever married. William himself died quite young when he was only 59 having been married for 32 years.

Sons:-

John the oldest son was born in 1721 and died in 1792 aged 71 years. In 1835 John's son Admiral Charles Adam received a knighthood from William IV. He died at Greenwich in 1853.

Robert 1728-92 (64 years). The famous architect.

James 1732-94 (62 years). Architect.

William 1738-1822 (84 years). Business-man.

Daughters:-

Susan married the 7th son of Sir John Clerk.

Mary married John Dryburgh from Kirkcaldy, a divine in Edinburgh.

Betty and Jenny kept house for Robert in London. Other sisters were **Nelly and Peggy.**

William Adam is buried in Greyfriars Kirkyard Edinburgh. The mausoleum was designed by his sons five years after his death.

Some of William Adam's Scottish Works

Forts:- Augustus, William and George.

General Wade's Bridge at Aberfeldy.

Taymouth and Floors Castles, Hopetoun, Dalmahoy. Newliston, Mellerstain, Arniston, Craigdarroch, Duff and The Drum houses.

REFERENCES "William Adam" by *James Simpson* for Scottish. Portrait Gallery 1985; "Kinross House", *N. Walker* 1990; "Robert Adam and his Circle" *John Fleming*, 1962; "Hopetoun House Guide".

Portrait of Robert Adam

ROBERT ADAM 1728-1792 (64 years)

Robert Adam's links with Kirkcaldy stem from the fact that he was born in Gladney House in the Linktown of Abbotshall and that for a very short time (1734-39) he was a pupil at the Burgh School, then in Hill Street.

Robert Adam was the son of William Adam and Mary Robertson of Gladney House, in the Linktown of Abbotshall. William Adam, his father, was an architect/builder and businessman in his own right and had started up the Brick and Tile Works in Linktown with William Robertson, Mary's father. This business eventually phased into the Methvens' Linktown Pottery. Remains of the Pottery buildings can be seen in Methven Road on the south side, the high walled building used now by the Body Zone Gym.

Robert Adam was born in 1728 in Gladney House, the second son of William Adam and Mary Robertson. There were four sons, John, Robert, James and William and six daughters, Jenny, Mary, Nelly, Peggy, Betty, and Susan. John was the only son to marry and Susan and Mary the only daughters.

After the first few years of schooling for Robert at the Burgh School in Hill Street, Kirkcaldy, the family moved to Edinburgh and Robert and his brothers continued their education at the High School in Edinburgh.

Robert went to Edinburgh University in 1743 aged 15 (not uncommon in those days to be a university student at so young an age). However he left without graduating owing to all the upsets with the '45 Uprising. He then joined his father and older brother John in the business of building and architecture. For the next eight years with his father (who died in 1748) and John, he was involved in the additions to Hopetoun House and building Fort George, near Nairn, the latter taking up much of his time during the summer months from 1748-1754.

William Adam, Robert's father died in 1748 and the inheritance passed to John. After William died Robert and James, Robert's younger brother, were involved with Fort George.

Building Restored by Robert Adam, Kinross

In 1754 it was time for Robert to broaden his interests and a Grand Tour of Europe was planned by him. He left for London and Europe in 1754 and returned in 1758, having spent most of his time in Italy mainly in Rome, enjoying not only the architecture but the life of the Grand Tourist. James continued the Fort George involvement during the summer months.

Unlike his father who built up his reputation solely on his own skills and by recommendation, Robert, though hard-working and highly talented, was a social climber and was desperate to get introductions into high society as he believed these were the only people with the money to spend on these grand schemes. He also obviously enjoyed mingling with the well-to-do and enjoyed the company of women. However he was determined to succeed in his own education and was not lured into matrimony.

His Grand Tour started with Charles Hope, the younger brother of Lord Hopetoun of Hopetoun House. Charles had plenty of connections, and Robert had the money. James Adam started out with them but left them in Paris. While Robert knew some French there were problems at the start with the Italian language. The French people bored Robert with their coldness and passion for cards, lacking in culture as he saw it, but he warmed straight away to the Italians despite any initial language difficulties.

Robert studied hard in Italy although the summer heat was very exhausting for there was no easy way to keep cool in those days but to leave the city. He made many drawings including a famous measured drawing of Diocletian's Palace at Spalatro (Dalmatia) and got many ideas from his Tour.

Robert also had an eye for good paintings, unlike his brother James, and he brought home from his Grand Tour a large collection of statues and paintings which he sold for a good sum.

All that remains of the Adelphi, now Royal Society of Arts.

James's Grand Tour would come later in 1760 but James was a dilettante enjoying the good life, spending money and not being inclined to hard work. Much of his "success" was in the shadow of Robert. Little that James started was ever finished.

To James was later left a tour of Greece, which Robert had not managed to include, in order to get new ideas but alas war in Europe and lack of sufficient pioneering spirit defeated James and Greece was never visited by any of the Adam brothers. (Seven Years War 1756-63)

However James's great purchase was on the order of his brother Robert to buy for King George III, the collecticn of paintings owned by the ailing Cardinal Albani. a friend of Robert's. This with great tact and diplomacy he succeeded in doing. These paintings are still in Windsor Castle today as part of the royal collection.

There were several different work periods within Robert Adam's life

1746-54 Worked with father (until 1748) and also brother John. James later joined the firm. (Robert aged 18-26 years)

1754-58 Grand Tour. About three and a quarter years (Robert aged 26-30 years).

1758-68 The London Life. The first year was slow to start and getting introductions to people that mattered took time. Robert set up house in London in Lower Grosvenor Street with his sisters Betty and Jenny. William also joined the family in London at this time. After one year life was still tough for Robert and he had been forced to ask John for a further loan. John was naturally a bit concerned. (Robert aged 30-40 years)

1768-74 MP for Kinross (age 40-46 years) This fitted in well with his London activities.

Post Grand Tour, London Robert wanted a public appointment to keep the finances straight and was soon involved in his first public building; the screen in front of the Admiralty building in London was his first major public works. In 1761 Robert was appointed jointly with William Chambers "Architect to the Kings Works".

Robert Adam's London Lodgings, John Adam Street.

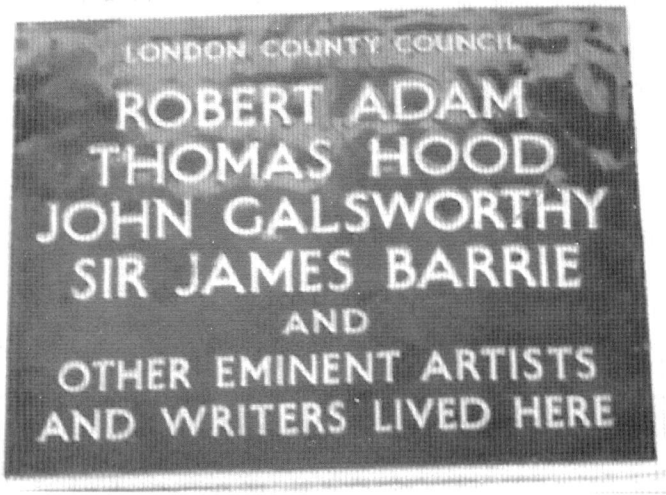

This post was passed on to James when Robert relinquished it in 1768. It was said that the only architect whom Robert feared was William Chambers. However when he met him and found him working in a garret he felt that he was in the lead. Robert was insanely jealous of all competition.

Robert meanwhile continued designing private houses and gardens on a grand scale. He specialised not only in lavish exteriors but in lavish interiors and furniture to go with it. One of the finest is Mellerstain, where he rebuilt the centre block between the two wings, designed by his father. Up and down the country Adam houses are still on view today, although sadly some like Mavisbank are awaiting funds, while others have already gone under the bulldozer.

By 1764 the Adam brothers company controlled timber, brickworks and stoneworks. At one time the firm, trading under the name of "William Adam and Co.", employed 2000-3000 designers and draughtsmen, many coming from the Continent. Kedlestone House, Osterley, Stowe to name a few are some of the big houses and estates designed by Robert Adam in England.

He had big plans for a water front development in London, the Adelphi for which the brothers took the lease for land in 1772. The word 'adelphi' is Greek for 'brothers'. The project never fully materialised due to cash-flow problems and the firm of William Adam and Co was close to bankruptcy. Items had to be sold off by lottery. Today one building remains in John Adam Street, London, the Royal Society of Arts.

In 1764 Robert published his first book on the "Ruins of the Palace of the Emperor Diocletian at Spalatro" (Dalmatia). This immediately became a best seller. Later the "Works in Architecture of Robert and James Adam" Volume 1 1772, Volume 2 1778 and Volume 3 1822 were published by William and were very popular.

There were so many works in Scotland for which the firm was commissioned that a new Edinburgh office was set up in 1772. After 1775 the Adams empire in England started to decline as the wars left

ROBERT ADAM Esquire

Architect

born at Kirkcaldie

3rd July 1728

died in London

3rd March 1792

Wording on his stone on the floor of Poets Corner, Westminster Abbey.

Plaque in Greyfriars Church. Edinburgh

people short of cash and unwilling to splurge on costly new buildings due to the American War of Independence (1775-76) and the scarcity of timber. After Robert died the firm of William Adam and Co. went bankrupt.

Work continued on many houses in Scotland, especially in Edinburgh. The designs however were not as lavish as those of the English Adam Houses. Robert's designs were very extravagant both inside and out and included items of furniture. Only people with a lot of money could afford the best. Robert had great talent and had been much influenced by his Grand Tour which might have been even richer had he travelled in Greece also.

Robert died suddenly in London in 1792 aged only 64 from a burst blood vessel in the stomach. One week later he was buried in Westminster Abbey. Two hundred years after his death, in 1992, a memorial plaque was unveiled in Greyfriars Church, Edinburgh.

Only the oldest of the Adam brothers married. But the brothers were not dry old bachelors. Robert certainly liked the good life and the "top drawer" people. He fell in love with an English lady at the end of his Grand Tour but alas she was looking after an ailing sister and was not prepared for serious wooing.

James four years younger was even more interested in making a good impression on people. He did not have the skill or the motivation of Robert and much of his work was mirrored from Robert's. Like Robert he was devoted to his mother and sisters and all were truly heartbroken when their mother died while James was on his Grand Tour in 1762. James died in 1794

William who was more a business man and never highly successful at that, died in London in 1822, having been looked after by his nieces. He was 10 years younger than Robert and lived over twenty years longer than his brothers or his father and I suspect his sisters as when he died he was cared for by nieces. William does not seem to have had artistic talent but was employed as the Manager of "William Adam and Co" and was also involved in ventures such as trying to import Spanish wines.

John was a talented architect but he did not have the advantage of the Grand Tour. John, however made a name for himself with landscape gardening and running the Estate at Blairadam. He died in 1792, six months after Robert. To him the Estate was bequeathed and through him the name continues in Keith Adam, the present owner and inhabitant. John was the one who had to find funds for various ventures of the other brothers.

In 1776 John Adam sold the family interests in the Brick and Tile Works in Linktown to David Methven whose son John developed the Pottery in 1810. There were very strong bonds of family closeness among the Adam family and a good sense of humour was shared by them all. Affectionately known as Bob to the family, Robert faithfully wrote home each week to his mother and his sisters. These letters have survived and tell us much about the man, his adventures and ideas.

In Kirkcaldy the only memorial to this "Son of Kirkcaldy" is in the plaque erected by Kirkcaldy Civic Society at Gladney Square, the new flats built close to the site of Gladney House.

It may be that St Brycedale House later known as the Hunter Hospital, was built from an Adam design in 1785 but there is no documentation to prove this. Certainly the interior shape of some of the rooms, the fireplaces and staircase give a distinct Adam atmosphere and style. A similar theory holds for Viewforth Tower, built around 1790, an Adam-like mansion, in Links Street where the multi-storey flats are today.

Viewforth Tower

Some of Robert Adam's Scottish works
Edinburgh.
> Charlotte Square
> General Register House.
> Old College, University of Edinburgh
> 7, Queen Street
> West Register House
> Part of the South Bridges

REFERENCES
"Robert Adam and his Circle", *John Fleming* 1962
"The Works of Robert Adam", *Geoffrey Beard* 1978
"Robert Adam's Country Houses", *Geoffrey Beard* 1981
"Born in Kirkcaldy", *D P Thomson*. 1852
"Scottish Men of Letters: Robert Adam", FRSE *Colin C. MacLean*

St Brycedale House now Hunter House

All that remains of Mavisbank (Wm Adam)

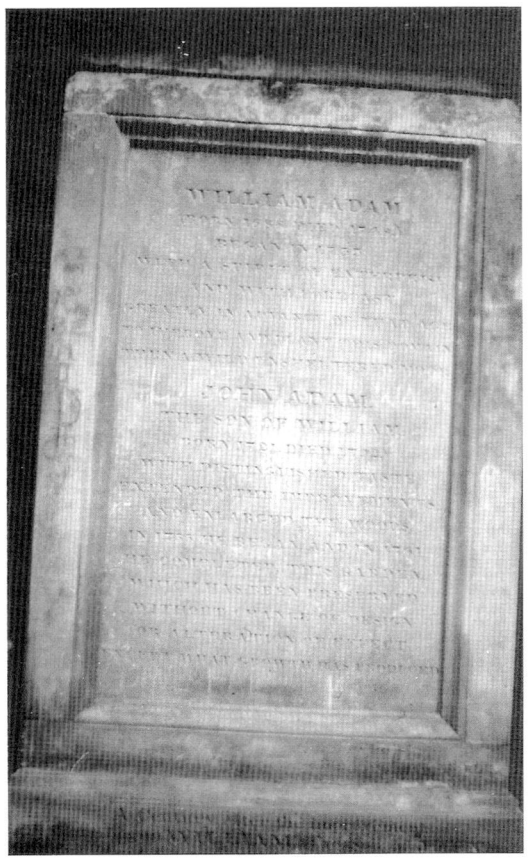

Monument in the Arboretum at Blairadam House

WILLIAM ADAM
BORN IN 1688 DIED 1748
BEGAN IN 1735
WITH SPIRIT AND ENTERPRISE
AND A FORECAST
GREATLY IN ADVANCE OF THAT AGE
TO IMPROVE AND PLANT THIS DOMAIN
THEN A WILD AND UNSHELTERED MOOR
JOHN ADAM
SON OF WILLIAM
BORN 1721 DIED 1792
WITH DISTINGUISHED TASTE
EXTENDED THE IMPROVEMENTS
AND ENLARGED THE WOODS.
IN 1733 HE BEGAN AND IN 1761
HE COMPLETED THIS GARDEN
WHICH HAS BEEN PRESERVED
WITHOUT CHANGE OF DESIGN
OR ALTERATION OF EFFECT
EXCEPT WHAT
GROWTH HAS PRODUCED.

A Century after the improvements were begun, William, son of John, aged 62, composed this inscription and placed it here in AD 1833.

The monument is listed.

Marjory from a drawing by Isobel Keith when she was 6 years old.

MARJORY FLEMING
1803-11 aged 8 years 11 months

Marjory Fleming was born at 130 High Street Kirkcaldy on January 15th 1803, the third child and the second daughter of James and Isabella Fleming.

Her father was an accountant who came to Kirkcaldy in 1788 from Kirkmichael in Perthshire. His father, Marjory's grandfather, had fought with Bonnie Prince Charlie at the Battle of Culloden in 1745.

James Fleming had been educated first at Blairgowrie, later at Perth Grammar School and then on to Edinburgh University. He came to Kirkcaldy because he had a brother Dr Thomas Fleming, who was the minister at St Brisse Church (Old Parish Church) in 1788, but who left Kirkcaldy in 1806 and went to Lady Yester's Church in Edinburgh.

Here in the Whyte House, at a ball given by Mr Walter Fergus, Provost and Chief Magistrate of Kirkcaldy, James Fleming met Isabella Rae, youngest daughter of an eminent Edinburgh Surgeon. She had two older brothers and an older sister Marianne who married William Keith and lived in Edinburgh. Isabella had been educated at the High School in Edinburgh.

Whyte House, demolished 2008

James and Isabella Rae were married at the old mansion house Giles of Grange, Edinburgh, the home of her grandfather and came to live in Kirkcaldy in 1797.

From Kirkcaldy Burgh Records we know that James Fleming was in 1791 and 1803 elected stentmaster (collector of various taxes). In 1796 he was elected Councillor and in 1797 became a Magistrate.

At first the Flemings lived in the Lion's House in Linktown. This was then described as "a curious old house with stone lions on pillars at the door". Later they moved to 130 High Street (now known as 132 High Street).

130 High Street was then a three storey house and there was a pend to the side, leading off from the High Street with a garden which ran down to the sea from the storm gable. The dining and drawing rooms were on the first floor with the drawing room overlooking the sea and the dining room overlooking the High Street. On the ground floor was a book shop. Through the pend lived the Heron family whose daughter Isabella was the same age as Marjory and indeed they often played together.

From 1914-1920 the Kirkcaldy Naturalists ran part of the building as a Marjory Fleming Museum. When this closed in 1920 we are told that some items were donated to Kirkcaldy Museum and others were returned to members of the families who had loaned them.

The house remained almost unchanged until 1920 when the inside was gutted to turn it into A K Melville, Ladies and Gents Outfitters, which closed in 1985. The house now numbered 132 is Holland and Barrett's Health Food shop. The nearby pend was closed around 1950 and a shop built into the little space. The back of 132 is rarely seen but it is little changed from Marjory's time, nearly 200 years ago. Indeed the house is over 300 years old. (See "Story of a Kirkcaldy House.") 132 has recently been listed.

On the first floor ceiling today, the room divisions can be seen and the place where the front door used to open out to the pend from the stairs was visible until the most recent internal alterations.

From both the upper floor windows Marjory delighted in watching all that was happening in the street below or on the Firth of Forth. The Nursery was on the upper floor and we are told that there was a gate to prevent her falling down or rolling down the stairs uninvited.

Mrs Fleming undertook the education for her daughters. Marjory had always had access to books and was encouraged to read and especially to read her Bible. She mastered the art of reading when she was just over three yeas old, having been desperate to read. Many of the books that children were encouraged to read at this time were rather boring books on morals and codes of conduct, the Bible and the Catechism.

At 130 High Street Marjory lived, for the first five years of her life, with her brother William, five years older, and her sister Isabella two years older, Elizabeth, the youngest, was born in 1809 when Marjory was just six years old.

Marjory was obviously a very clever child and full of energy and creative ideas, pranks and temper tantrums. Books were important in the family and Marjory was read to and learned to read and write before she was four years old. She was a well-built healthy little girl with much desire for adventure and mischief, with a temper and very much a mind of her own.

A story is told concerning Marjory and her high spirits, of a happening when she was out for a walk with her sister and elderly nursemaid Jeannie Robertson, in the grounds of Raith near the Mill Dam (there was no Beveridge Park in those days). Marjory impulsively ran on ahead and the nurse, afraid she might fall into the water, shouted to her but she paid no heed, Isabella was sent after her. Marjory fell and would have fallen into the water and probably been drowned if her sister had not grabbed her by her clothes. She saved Marjory, but her dress was badly torn. The nurse scolded Isabella but Marjory beseeched her not to scold her sister who had saved her life, "not Isabella" she exclaimed "or I shall roar like a bull", Marjory and Jeannie often came to blows.

Marjorie's House when she lived here. Rear today, unchanged.

Front today with a plaque

Another time she ran into the wet garden and when her sister was sent to look for her, hid in the bushes. These stories were told again and again with visits to the Raith Lake long after Marjory had died.

When Marjory was five and a half years old there was a visit from her 17 year old cousin Isabella or Isa Keith from Edinburgh. lsa and Marjory formed an instant bond of affection. At this time Mrs Fleming was expecting another child who was born when Marjory was just six in 1809. Isa suggested that perhaps it would be a good idea if Marjory could accompany her back to Edinburgh. It was the summer of 1808.

This she did travelling with Isa by stage-coach to Kinghorn and by ferry across to Leith and so on to Edinburgh. It must be remembered that in those days the journey to Edinburgh was quite a hazardous one and was not to be lightly undertaken as it is today and sometimes the seas were very rough. In Edinburgh Mrs Keith lived at 1, North Charlotte Street. Mrs Keith's family, two sons William and CharIes and two daughters, Isabella and Nancy, were all older than Marjory. Grandfather Keith had a big house at Ravelston, now demolished.

Marjory had had quite a simple upbringing and Marjory's nurse Jeannie was old and bad tempered and had other household duties than just the children. In contrast the Edinburgh house and its life style was much grander, the clothes that the family wore were smarter and there were more servants. But then such a life style might look out of place in Kirkcaldy. Animals were a part of many houses at this time and the Keiths had lots of caged birds and there were dogs and cats.

Isa, although only 17 took personal responsibility for the upbringing and education of Marjory at this time. Isa set her to keep a Journal. It is this that has been preserved and has given us so much information about the conditions of children in those days and the thoughts that could pass through the mind of a child. Thus Marjory was given a book in which she could write her thoughts and experiences, but which lsabella would read later to correct the grammar and spelling.

Braehead, below now; above in Marjory's time

A correspondence later developed between Marjory and her older sister Isabella in Kirkcaldy, although Marjory was reluctant to start as she hated letter writing and at five and a half who can blame her. It was dipping pens in those days and a laborious task to write a neat and legible letter.

It is quite remarkable that Marjory had such an adult command of English with many very long words which she spelt in the phonetic way. The Journal was indeed a much more interesting task than the boring old grammar and spelling books. However some of the long words that Marjory used were mimicked from listening to adults, not fully knowing the meaning they were often inappropriate.

Marjory was taught about many of the great poets and writers, Shakespeare, Walter Scott, Pope and Gray. She listened to stories about Mary, Queen of Scots, about whom she wrote a very long poem and another about James VI. In between Isabella told stories about people in history and the Bible was read every day. Her horizons were broadened by outside visits and excursions such as visiting a travelling menagerie. An Exhibition of paintings in Edinburgh which opened in 1810 intrigued Marjory and she wanted to see them but it was expensive. She also wanted to go to the theatre.

Marjory is thus described at this time by Isa:- "She has grown excessively fat and strong but I cannot say she is great in beauty".

The other source of knowledge about Marjory and her times, apart from the poems and Journals, were the letters she wrote to her mother and her sister, although she was very reluctant to do so at the beginning. However when she returned to her own home two years later she wrote frequently to Isa, at times much to the annoyance of her mother who must have been jealous of the affection and devotion to Isa.

Marjory's writing when she arrived in Edinburgh left a lot to be desired. Isa hoped that writing the Journal would be good practice and would interest her little pupil. This methodology at this time was unconventional, but it certainly formed the correct motivating force for Marjory. Arithmetic was not a favourite subject and music and dancing were really disliked. At first two to three hours a day were spent in lessons and by the following year about three to four hours.

Much of Isa's summer times were spent at Braehead, the house at Cramond, which is still there. Braehead is described by Marjory as "a sweet place in a charming situation beside woods and rivulets". The house was owned by a Mrs Crauford and the two families were very friendly. Around this time Isa's brother William married Mrs Crauford's daughter Isabella.

At Braehead Marjory slept in the same bed as Isa. Often she woke early desperate to start the day while Isa slept on. At the start of her first summer at Braehead Marjory started her Second Journal. Now she dated the entries and the facts were more organised. Marjory was often bad tempered and even threw things at Isa. Afterwards she was sorry and was continually upset by her own inability to control her temper. Isa dealt with her by sending her to her room to pray.

Ravelston House, in Murrayfield was another house visited frequently by Marjory. Here lived Isa's grandfather Keith. This house was dated 1672. Sir Walter Scott friend and relative of the Keith's played here frequently as a boy and continued to visit as an adult. William Keith's first cousin was Walter Scott's father. Walter Scot certainly visited the Keiths as well as being related, but how often he met Marjory during her two year stay is uncertain for she does not mention meeting him in her Journals although she mentions his works and he does not mention her in his writings.

In her Journals Marjory describes a number of gruesome events of the day; the soldier dying on the battlefield; the man Hartman and his 10 sons publicly hanged; the maid who tried to poison her mistress and children and about many deportations. She is also horrified to find that the unwanted progeny of cats and dogs were being drowned.

Marjory's uncle the Reverend Fleming had left Kirkcaldy in 1806 to take up a post in Lady Yester's Presbyterian Church. However while in

Edinburgh Marjory did not attend her Uncle's Church but accompanied her cousins to the Episcopal Church.

A note from Isa Keith states at the end of the Second Journal that "Marjory must write no more journals until she writes better". The Third Journal was written when Marjory was seven and started in the spring of 1810. At one point during her stay in Edinburgh her father came to visit her.

Marjory's new sister was born early in 1809 and until her mother felt able to cope, Marjory did not return home. Her mother sent for her in July 1811 and with great sadness and reluctance Marjory returned home but she was never again the carefree child she had been before she left home or while she was staying in Edinburgh.

Marjory's mother sent for her when Elizabeth, the new baby was already two years old. Isa Keith and Marjory were both devastated at having to part but Marjory was a Fleming and she belonged to Kirkcaldy. She had been very happy in Edinburgh where she was the centre of attention and was more often treated as a young adult. She never seemed to miss Kirkcaldy.

Marjory returned home in July 1811 aged eight and a half, heartbroken at leaving Isa and the life she had fitted into so well in Edinburgh. She never saw any of the Keiths again. She sailed on her own from Leith to Kinghorn where her father met her.

Life at home was very strange for a while and she pined for Edinburgh and Isa's love and companionship. William Fleming was now 13, Isabella 11 and the new baby Elizabeth over two years old.

Marjory continued her lessons at home with her mother as the teacher, but frequently she let out and shouted about the stupid books. On one occasion this led her mother to forbid her to talk about Edinburgh or Isa again. Marjory was humiliated at the outburst, hurt about her mother's reaction and bottled up her feelings.

"I am now in my native land
And see my dear friends all at hand
There is a thing that I do want
With you these beauteous walks to haunt
We would be happy if you would
Try to come over if you could
Then I would quite happy be".

She wrote and complained when she got no reply:-
"Oh Isa why do you not write to me
I'm out of mind when out of sight
I am afraid you are dead and gone
And this I so be in my mood
O miserable unhappy child
To lose a mistress meek and mild".

Marjory's second memorial stone.   KCS plaque at main entrance

Mrs Fleming arranged that the 13 year old William should spend some time at Braehead. Marjory was furious and extremely jealous. That was almost too much for Marjory's self control.

Much against her wishes Marjory was persuaded to join her sister and Isabella Heron at dancing classes and indeed the children spent much time playing together. On this particular day in September Isabella Heron was unable to go to the dancing class because she had measles. Isabella and Marjory then said that Isabella Heron had been 'hot and cold' the last time they played with her. In a letter to Isa she says that measles is raging all around and Isabella Heron had nearly died of it.

Shortly afterwards Marjory was found with a fever, Marjory had measles. Her convalescence was long and slow as summer went and winter came again.

>"O Isa do remember me
>
>And try to love your Marjory".

Her last poem three days before she died was written just before she lost consciousness:-

>"Oh Isa pain did visit me
>
>I was at the last extremity
>
>How often did I think of you
>
>I wished your graceful form to view
>
>To clasp you in my weak embrace
>
>Indeed 1 thought I'd run my race
>
>Good care I'm sure was of me taken
>
>But still indeed I was much shaken
>
>At last I daily strength did gain
>
>And oh! at last away went pain.

> At length the doctor thought I might.
>
> Stay in the parlour all the night
>
> I now continue so to do
>
> Farewell to Nancy and to you ".

She awoke during the night with a splitting headache and cried out "My head my head". Those were her last words before she lapsed into unconsciousness. She died three days later of meningitis ("water on the brain").

Marjory Fleming was buried in Abbotshall Churchyard, with a simple stone "MF 1803-11". Later (after 1850) a marble cross was erected to "Pet Marjorie". This name was given to her by Dr John Brown in his book of 1850. In 1937 a special stone was erected on the back of the original stone and in red granite Marjory Fleming sits reading a book.

Originally a small plaque had been on one of the main gate pillars of Abbotshall Kirkyard stating that "Author, poet and diarist Pet Marjorie is buried here", but it disappeared. In 1990 Kirkcaldy Civic Society placed a plaque near the main gate with the information *"Author, poet and diarist, Marjory Fleming ("Pet Marjorie") was buried here in 1811 aged 8 years, 11 months".*

Kirkcaldy Civic Society has also, in conjunction with the Hall of Cards, placed a plaque on the house where she was born and where she died at 132 High Street, *"Pet Marjorie, the youngest immortal in the world of letters Marjory Fleming. Born 15.1.1803. Died 19.12.1811"*

References

"Pet Marjorie" *Dr John. Brown* c 1860
"Story of Pet Marjorie" *L. Macbean* 1928
"The Complete Marjory Fleming, Her Journals, Letters and Verses", ……*Sidgwick* 1934
"The Journals and Poetry of Marjory Fleming" *Harriet Smyth* 1990
"Story of an Old Kirkcaldy House" *Helen K Bryson* 1911.
"Learn to Love your Marjory" Play *Harriet Smyth* c 1992.

Robert Philp's West Mill, demolished 2003.

ROBERT PHILP 1751 -1828

Robert Philp was born on March 28th 1751, in Kirkcaldy, the son of William Philp and Alison Heggie (or Haiggie).

His father was the son of James Philp and Katherine Imbrie, whose brother John was the grandfather of Dr John Philip, the missionary in South Africa. Alison Heggie, Robert Philp's mother was the daughter of James Haiggie, a merchant from Kinglassie.

William Philp, Robert's father was a merchant in Kirkcaldy. Robert was the oldest son, a second son James died when young and there were two sisters Isobel and Rachael, but we hear no more of them. We know little of Robert Philp's early life but he belonged to the merchant class and was probably educated at the Burgh School, which opened in 1725 in Hill Street.

Robert Philp died at the age of 77 in his country mansion house at Edenshead in 1828. Gateside is the name by which the old village of Edenshead is today known and there is a hotel in the village - the Edenshead Arms.

In 1824 at the age of 73, Robert Philp bought Pitlochie House in Edenshead or Gateside and lived there for four years before he died. During the short time that he was there he gave a piece of ground for a church to be built in Edenshead rather than the villagers having to walk all the way to Strathmiglo on a Sabbath morning, in order to worship.

When he died Robert Philp owned an extensive spinning, bleaching and dyeworks in Linktown of Abbotshall, near Kirkcaldy, known as the West Mill (Linktown did not join with the Burgh of Kirkcaldy until 1876). The mill depended on the water power of the Tiel Burn and was never converted to steam by Robert Philp.

Robert Philp in early years travelled all over Fife collecting linen from the home weavers. This he took to markets in towns like Perth and Dundee. Soon he found spinning and weaving was more profitable and

Linktown Philp School demolished 1964

Kirkcaldy Philp School, Charlotte Street

there was a greater output from factories so in 1815 he bought the West Mill with its bleachfield.

Robert Philp was a Merchant Councillor (1776-93) and later Bailie (1788-90) in the Burgh of Kirkcaldy where he lived until he moved to Edenshead. He worshipped at the Old Parish Church then known as St Brisse and is buried there.

He never married and as far as we know he had already fallen out with any relatives he had as some of them had changed their name from Philp to Philip. Robert Philp had been very angry when he heard about this and said "if ma name is na guid enough for them then neither is ma siller"! Robert Philp thus left his considerable estate, £70,000 in trust "for the education and clothing of poor children".

Robert Philp set up his trust eight years before he died, in 1820. In it he instructed, except for a few minor bequests, that his Estates be sold and the money invested for the education of poor children in Kirkcaldy and Kinghorn.

Some say that much of Robert Philp's fortune was made like many others at this time, by large investments in the West Indies and that these reaped a good profit because of the continuing traffic in slaves. The Emancipation Act was passed in Britain which included the Colonies, in 1839, thus officially ending slavery, but not unofficially.

Philp Schools were set up for children in Kirkcaldy, Linktown and Pathhead, with also provision for the education of 50 children from Kinghorn, the latter being later increased to 150 pupils. In the three areas of Kirkcaldy schools were built and were operational within five years of his death.

With the Education Act of 1872 Local Authority Board Schools were set up and the Philp Schools, not being taken over, were phased out and by 1891 were closed. The Philp Schools served the working classes well and many pupils, Philpers passed through the schools receiving education, clothing and books. In return on the anniversary of Robert

Philp's birthday in March there was a procession to his grave where each pupil deposited a rose and was later rewarded with a bun.

TO THE MEMORY OF
ROBERT PHILP
LINEN MANUFACTURER IN KIRKCALDY
Who died on the 14th April 1828 aged 77 years.
By attention to Business
And integrity in Dealing
He accumulated wealth
The most of which he destined
To form a permanent capital
The proceeds whereof to be
Applied in Educating and Clothing
Poor children and providing them
With a sum of money
For this laudable purpose
His funds were invested
On lands in the parishes of

£
Strathmiglo................20,000
Collessie..................10,200
Kinghorn 39,800
And on heritable bonds.700
70,700

In Linktown the school became a public hall and was replaced by the New Philp Hall, built in 1962 slightly further south and before the old building was demolished in 1967. In Sinclairtown the school was surrounded by the Nairn buildings and demolished with these buildings in the 1967. The Kirkcaldy Philp School which replaced an earlier education centre in Charlotte Street, remains as Caesars. (Until recently AfterDark, now Society). On the gate post Kirkcaldy Civic Society has placed a plaque to the memory of Robert Philp and his unique contribution to the children of Kirkcaldy.

Robert Philp's tombstone stands in the Old Parish Kirk with details of where his money had been invested which added up to over £70,000. In all the villages named Robert had had property and there were important mills.

There is still money available for schools from the Philp Trust within the West Fife Trust. This should be used for items not otherwise available from main funds ie like travel, or cameras.

References
"Robert Philp Trust".
"Bailie Robert Philp". Annie MacPhedran 1991
"Story of a Fife Family Part 1 and 2" Private publication. S. Africa

Pitlochie House in Edenshead now known as Gateside

Plaque on Old Kirkcaldy Philp School

The PHILPS or PHILIPS

John Philp 1634 married Euphan Birrell. Died 1649.

Son John Philp born 1635. In 1660 married Bessie Angus.

Son James Philp born 1665. In 1690 married Janet Wallace.

Son. James Philp born 1691. In 1716 married Katherine Imbrie.

(Son 1 John Philp born 1720.1749 married Mary Dougal (d. 1777).

(Son 2 William born 1726, father of Robert Philp.

Son of John was James 1750-1808. Married Eliz. Marshall. 1774

Son John 1775 later Dr John Philip, died South Africa 1851.

Dr John Philip's grandfather & Robert Philp's grand-uncle were cousins.

Robert Philp had no children. His brother James died young and of his two sisters Isobel and Rachael nothing more is known.

The children of James Philp (1750-1808) and Elizabeth Marshall :-

John	1775
James	1777
Helen and Rachael	1779
Oswald	1780
Thomas	1793

Dr John Philip, changed his name from Philp to Philip. He had seven children (one Margaret died when an infant) and many grandchildren, most of whom settled in South Africa. Only his daughter Mary had children who settled in England.

Bailie Robert Philp and Dr John Philip were 'distant cousins'.

JOHN PHILP or JOHN PHILIP 1775-1851

John Philp was born in Kirkcaldy on April 14th 1775 the son of James Philp 1750-1808 and Elizabeth Marshall 1752-1822.

James, John Philip's grandfather and William Philp's grand-uncle were cousins. John was a distant cousin of Robert. Robert Philp is said to have been present when John Philp was baptised in the Old Kirk in 1775. Robert would then have been 24 years old.

John Philp's parents are buried in the Old Parish Kirk graveyard, a stone marking their grave tells us that John Philp erected this memorial to his parents on one of his visits to Scotland. It was lying face down and it was decided when re-erected to note the wording on the plaque in case it can no longer be read.

Ann Watters, Albert Sommerville, Rev. John Reid and Rev. Dr McNaughton

"This stone was erected by Rev. John Phil(i)p, Missionary in South Africa in memory of his parents. His father John died in 1808 aged 58 and his mother Elizabeth Marshall in 1822 aged 70".

James Philp, grandfather of John was deacon of the Hammermen (smiths) 1742-44, quite an important position in the community. James, John's father was a skilled handloom weaver and was well read, owning several books.

John Philp was most probably educated at the Burgh School, which was in Hill Street from 1725-1843 after which it moved to a new building in St Brycedale Avenue. School finished when John was eleven and he was then apprenticed to his father's trade.

The family attended the Parish Church. The first Secession from the Church of Scotland had already taken place in 1733, resulting in the establishment of Bethelfield (now Linktown) Church.

At the age of fifteen John's distant cousin Robert Philp, who lived in Kirkcaldy and had many business interests in the West Indies, offered him a position there with a cotton growing and picking business, the labour of which was mostly done by slaves. John turned it down as he believed and knew his cousin was involved in the slave trade and such a practice was abhorrent to him. Slavery was not abolished until the passing of the Act of Emancipation 1839, in Britain and the Colonies and in America not until after the Civil War of 1861. John had been active in campaigning for this Bill.

During the years after leaving school John continued to read and attended evening classes at one of the newly opened 'Academies'. He was well known when still young for his ability to debate many moral issues of the day. One especially remembered was on "infidelity".

John Philp's first job was in a Leven spinning factory. There he stayed with an uncle who was one of the Glassites. Glassites or Sandemanians were Non-Conformists who had broken away from both the Established and the Secession Church; he was thus introduced to the new Non-Conformist movement.

In 1794 when he was 19 he was offered a post as a clerk in a Dundee spinning mill. He was soon found to be of quality material and became manager. When he went to Dundee he attended the 'Independent Chapel' which with the Haldane brothers' influence broke away from the Non-Conformists and separated from the Baptists as they believed in infant rather than adult baptism. He thus became a Congregationalist. The minister in Dundee who greatly influenced him was the Reverend Thomas Durant, who realised how John felt about child labour and other social injustices. He eventually persuaded John that his calling was in the ministry.

John Philp was shocked at the conditions he saw in the mills both in Fife and Dundee. Here children of nine years of age might be working a 12-14 hour day, six days a week. He spoke out about this blatant exploitation of child labour and eventually was sacked. He went back home to work with his father while waiting to come to a decision about his future. After 6 months, in 1799 aged 24, he applied for a place at Horton College in London and started his three year training for the Ministry.

Here he studied, spending much of his free time working with the poor and destitute in the slums of London.

When in Dundee and before going to London, he and his brother changed the spelling of their name from Philp to Philip, The reason for this may have been to make the name easier for the English tongues to pronounce.

When Robert Philp heard this he was very angry and when he died, a bachelor, he left all his money to the education of poor children in and around Kirkcaldy for he said . 'If ma name is na guid enough fa them then neither is ma siller".

Reverend John Philip's first charge in 1802 was as assistant minister in the Congregational Church in Newbury-on-Thames, Berkshire. Here he gained a great reputation. amongst the farmers for his Sunday evening lectures.

In 1804 when he was 29 he was called to the Congregational Church in Aberdeen and was their second minister. The congregation already had major differences of opinion and he spent two years trying to win over and unite the congregation. He was a very determined minister especially when he believed himself to be in the right. In desperation he dissolved his congregation, indeed a very radical step and re-formed with those who believed they could work with him. Of the 277 adult members of the congregation, 247 stayed and from then on the Church grew and prospered until it was filled with over 1200 people each Sunday.

One of his great contributions in Aberdeen was about the importance of young people and that included girls. Many mixed discussion groups were organised by him in the manse.

Here in Aberdeen he met Jane Ross. She was the daughter of an Aberdeen architect and she and her family had been converted by John Philip and in 1809 they were married.

John spent 14 years in Aberdeen and four children later he was persuaded to go for five years to Cape Town with James Campbell on behalf of the London Missionary Society to investigate how some of the mission stations were coping and to advise and improve them. He refused to accept the South African challenge until he was released by his Church, which it was most reluctant to do.

In 1818 John and Jane Ross sailed for South Africa, from Liverpool in the "Westmoreland" under Captain Cririe, with James Campbell and their two sons, William who was four and a half and John Ross who was two. The Philip's two older children, daughters Mary and Elizabeth stayed with the Reverend Thomas Durant, then in Poole in Dorset, in order to finish their education.

John Philip never returned to live in Britain, but did return for two visits. All his children settled in South Africa, with the exception of his daughter Mary who after rejoining the family, met and married Congregational Minister/ex-missionary George Christie while visiting Britain.

There are now many members of the Philip family in South Africa and in many other parts of the world. Peter Philip has written a book in two volumes, "A Fifeshire Family" with some details of the family history and its many members.

In Capetown John and Jane lived in the Mission House, in Church Square next to the Union Church. John Philp was the minister to that Congregational Union Church, as well as having the supervision of the missions as Resident Director of the London Missionary Society. He took many long and arduous journeys into the interior to visit the Mission Stations.

John Philip is described as a big man, over six feet tall. He had a pleasant and friendly face and laughter was never far away. He had beaming eyes and thick eyebrows. The family was a close and united one and often at meal times there was much laughter which at times shocked some of the more reserved missionaries.

He also championed the cause of the Hottentots, Khoi and Xhosa peoples who were being exploited as cheap labour. The Boers regarded him as a dangerous element who could ignite an uprising at any time. He believed in equal rights of all citizens regardless of colour.

John Philip was soon introduced to the practical aspects of the colour bar and the white supremacy of especially the Boers. He also realised that Slavery was part of the culture in South Africa and many farmers were dependent on the cheap labour thus provided. He believed that the abolition of Slavery and pseudo-slavery, with the removal of education, trade and land ownership barriers this would help all aspects of the economic development of the country for the benefit of all.

He was determined to see slavery abolished in all British colonies and he had allies at Westminster in William Wilberforce and later with Thomas Fowell Buxton, leaders of the Anti-Slavery Society. Slavery was finally abolished in law, if not in practice, in 1839 by the passing of the Act of Emancipation.

Many missionaries passing through Cape Town, of all nationalities stayed at the Mission House, including Robert Moffat and David Livingstone in 1841. David Livingstone was said to have remarked that he was rather dreading his stay there. He stayed a month in the end, but ended up really admiring and enjoying the atmosphere of the Philip household.

Jane was said to be an ideal wife and accepted life in Africa as a great challenge. She supported her husband in so much but always kept herself in the background. She was indeed the hub of the wheel that the family revolved around. She was also the unofficial treasurer of the London Missionary Society in South Africa and from 1830 until her death in 1847 she was the official agent of the Paris Evangelical Mission in South Africa.

Three more children were born in South Africa, in 1819 Thomas Durant, in 1825 a daughter Margaret who sadly did not live for long Finally in 1829 Wilberforce Buxton, named after the two chief British activists in the abolition of Slavery.

In 1819 John Philip received an Honorary Doctorate from Columbia University and in 1820 a similar one from Princeton, both in absentia.

In 1826 John returned to England to raise funds and to fight for the Abolition of Slavery. Shortly after he left, the Governor of South Africa Lord Charles Somerset was recalled to London for mishandling matters. He and Philip had clashed on many occasions.

Dr John Philip returned to South Africa in 1829 to a period of being a good friend of the new Governor and had some successes in his dealings on behalf of the African tribes. Some have called him from his work of this period the 'Protestant Pope of South Africa' and others 'Elijah of South Africa'.

The Mackay libel case was brought against him shortly after his return from Britain. Mackay was a local official who found Philip's democratic outlook dangerous. Philip's witnesses were Khoi, who when it came to the trial amounted to only two who were prepared to act as witnesses in court. One was so scared that his replies were discredited, and the other was not deemed fit to witness. Philip lost the case and was ordered to pay £200 damages and £400 costs which of course he could not afford to pay. The fines were finally paid for him by the London Missionary Society.

In 1836 he also returned to Britain for two years this time taking a Hottentot and a Kaffir with him to help to raise money for the missions. There was a serious Kaffir rebellion while he was away.

He rightly believed that fairness and sincerity in all dealings with African and Cape people is what makes for peace. Unfortunately so often there was greed and treachery by both the British and the Boer settlers. Cattle were stolen from the blacks, land was "acquired" by the whites, treaties broken by the whites and always it was the white man's word against the black man. This bred anger and discontent and did not go well for good race relations.

Dr John Philip was very upset about the Great Trek of 1835. Here the Boers set off to establish a country of their own, free from Britain and British interference. On their wanderings they met in the north the Zulus, whose chief warrior was Dingaan. While "trusting and treatying" the Boers were murdered by the Zulus, for they were marching north to acquire more Zulu-land. So many of the African tribes had been betrayed. There had been the "Battle of the Axe" when the Khoi were betrayed after being accused of stealing an axe.

At times many African tribesmen were forced into army service and given no pay, issued only with a blanket and rations and at the end of the service were expected to return the blanket! While they were away their families could not always manage the harvest unaided. Once again exploitation of the black Africans.

Dr John Philip did so much for South African equality, but towards the end of his life he felt completely betrayed by events.

Tragically his son William and grandson were drowned in 1845 and his wife Jane, his soul mate died in 1847, another grandson son of his daughter Mary (in England) and the Reverend George Christie died in a tragic accident in 1847.

In 1849 he retired at the age of 74 and in 1851 he died in Hankey, South Africa at the home of his son Thomas Durant. His daughter Mary, from England, was looking after him while her husband George Christie, a Congregational minister/missionary was engaged on a two year tour of the South African missions. The last six years of his life were most traumatic and he must have felt that all that he had tried to achieve was falling apart, even the missionaries had turned against him. However the 'Cape Coloureds' did achieve their vote at about this time only to have it later removed.

Half a century after his death, came the Boer Wars, later still the Laws of Apartheid and again later the forming of a Republic. All this occurred before the statesman Mandela emerged after 26 years in jail, without bitterness, to lead the nation into universal black and white suffrage. One awaits the future with hope and interest.

Some have wondered who could have carried on Dr John Philip's great mission for African equality, only one man and that was David Livingstone. Alas at about that time he was leaving for the interior of Africa and never returned again to South Africa.

Today after nearly 150 years Dr John Philip would have been delighted to see that all people dwelling in South Africa now have the vote, regardless of colour.

William Philip

William (1814) went to University in Britain in 1826, but he was not happy and ran away to sea, boarded a whaler at 19. Soon the Captain died of apoplexy so he found himself taking charge of the whaler. In 1833 he left the sea and returned to Cape Town, later going back to Glasgow to train for the Ministry. Here he met Alison Bell who became his 18 year-old wife in 1840. They sailed back to Cape Town. She was very beautiful and in her mother-in-law's words, she did not appear suitable. She proved to be a tower of strength, nursing smallpox cases when only 19, shortly after giving birth to their first child.

William went to the Cambrian Mission in South Africa and gained the distinction of producing the best irrigation scheme, in his area. The tunnel of the scheme became a National Monument. Tragically William at 31 drowned in 1845 trying to save his 10 year old nephew, Johnny Fairbairn from drowning. (Elizabeth's son). Alison his widow married again, one Andrew Muir who was a Merchant in Moscow. Tragedy struck again and her son Walter with Andrew perished during the Russian Revolution.

John Ross and Thomas Durant

The second son, John Ross and the third son Thomas also went home to finish their education at Mill Hill. John Ross returned to Cape Town and started a printing and publishing business.

Thomas Durant named after the Rev. Thomas Durant, was the first member of the family born in South Africa and went to Glasgow University after Mill Hill, training to be a Missionary, qualifying in 1844. He returned to work in South Africa and decided to work in the area where William, his brother had recently died. He was married twice to Louisa Jane Silberbauer and to Jane Margaret Hughes.

Wilberforce Buxton

Wilberforce Buxton was the youngest of the family and was named after the two men in Britain who campaigned effectively for the Abolition of Slavery. Like his brothers he went to school in London and later trained for the ministry and became a missionary to the tough Griquas. He married his cousin Susanna Field Fisher and two of his sons pioneered in Rhodesia founding a firm A Philip and Co.

Daughters Mary and Elizabeth.

Mary and Elizabeth travelled to South Africa after they had finished their schooling. Mary married John Fairbairn, a Scottish missionary who worked very closely with John Philip and after John died achieved a limited franchise for the Cape folk (coloureds).

Elizabeth, on a visit to Britain met George Christie a Congregational minister/ex-missionary and settled in England. However she and her husband visited South Africa on a two year tour of the Missions in 1849 and she was looking after her father when he died.

References
"Born in Kirkcaldy". *D.P. Thomson* 1952.
"John Philip 1775-1851, Missions, Race & Politics in South Africa". *Andrew Ross* 1986.
"A Fifeshire Family". Vol. 1 and 2 *Peter Philip* 1975.
    Private publication

Sir SANDFORD FLEMING 1827-1915

Sandford Fleming was born in Kirkcaldy in Glasswork Street on the 7th of January 1827. The family cabinet-making and upholstery business was in Cowan Street and the family later moved to 'West Park' in Rose Street.

Sandford was the son of Andrew Greig Fleming of Kennoway and Elizabeth Arnot. His father was the son of David Fleming and Janet Greig. It was said that the McGregors after the massacre of Glencoe fled to Kennoway and changed their name to Greig. Andrew Fleming and his brother Alexander ran a cabinet-making and upholsterer's business, originally in Kennoway, before moving to the Links in 1824 when they bought a similar business from the late Mr William Mitchell. There were eight children in the family. Sandford was named after an uncle of the same name and another who was a renowned sanskrit scholar who lived in India. His mother's grandfather was a Cameron who had fought at Culloden and who had helped to return Bonnie Prince Charlie to France.

Six early school years were spent at Kennoway School where a Mr Bethune was the teacher, Sandford was staying with his paternal grandparents, which was a common practice in those days. Bethune later emigrated to Canada and was there to welcome David and Sandford Fleming on their arrival at Montreal in 1845. The rest of Sandford's education was at the Burgh School in Kirkcaldy which was in Hill Street until 1843.

Christianity and the Church were very important to all the family and remained so in Sandford's life right up until the end. The family probably attended the Old Parish Church.

Sandford studied engineering and surveying and was apprenticed to John Sang Engineers and Surveyors, Kirkcaldy, when he was 14 years old (1841). Sangs were at that time engaged in extending the harbour, building railways and developing water works. Later the firm surveyed the extended Burgh 1879-80. His brother David who was two years older was a cabinet maker at that time in the family business.

Sandford Fleming kept a diary from his earliest years and so we have his candid account of many events and happenings of the times. The journals are now held in the National Museum of Canada.

In 1844 a cousin of the family who had emigrated to Canada, paid the Flemings a visit. He was Henry Hutchison, a Doctor, from Peterborough, Ontario. Here the first seeds of the idea about emigrating were planted as Dr Hutchison suggested that the two brothers, David a wood carver and Sandford an engineer and surveyor should emigrate to Canada and set things up so that the rest of the family could follow later. Business was not too healthy in Kirkcaldy at that time.

David, Sandford and cousin Henry left Kirkcaldy on April 24th 1845 and sailed from Glasgow on the 'Brilliant' for a six week voyage to Canada. Sandford reports in his diary that the journey was stormy and their quarters were filthy. People were sick and the stench was unbearable. It was not a pleasant experience. The journey was very dangerous and there were genuine fears that the ship would not make port. Sandford was so concerned "18 is too young to die" that despite the weather he wrote his father a letter, placed it in a bottle and threw it into the rough sea. Fortunately the good news of his arrival reached his father before the letter in the bottle which took seven months !

When the brothers reached Montreal they were met by their old Kennoway teacher Mr Bethune who had gone to Canada as a missionary, but who was shortly moving further in to the interior of the country. They continued their journey with him in a steamer up the St Lawrence to Toronto from where they made their way to Peterborough to Dr Hutchison's house.

Sandford stayed two months with his distant cousin and often went on his rounds with him. Eventually he and David went to Toronto to look for jobs, where David quickly got work, but not Sandford.

Mr Bethune had a small farm close to Dr Hutchison but he was shortly to move to a new farm further inland. Sandford helped in the removal as he had no job at that time. People were advising him to go home, which he had no intention of doing and in desperation he nearly became a farm manager.

Soon he heard that Dr Hutchison was very ill and unlikely to recover and he went back to see what he could do. At this time Sandford took many meals across the road in the home of James Hall a friend of Henry Hutchison. Here he became acquainted with Jean Hall then 14. But Dr Hutchison recovered and continued on his rounds and was able to find a humble job for Sandford as a draughtsman. Sadly in 1838 he contracted typhoid fever from some of the Irish immigrants living nearby and died. His widow and children went to live in Toronto. In recognition of his thanks Sandford planted a weeping willow tree over Dr Henry Hutchison's grave. Dr Hutchison's house has now become a Museum and has a Fleming Room.

Dr Hutchison's house has become a Museum and has a Fleming room.

Sandford was a big man, six feet tall with auburn hair which later went pure white. He always carried about with him a burning enthusiasm for life with boundless energy. He had a kind and gentle face. He was a very determined man and one night missing the train home he decided to walk along the track, visibility was poor and he had kept his head down to make sure he was on the track. Suddenly he looked up and he was face to face with a large bear. The only weapon he had to hand was his umbrella. This he shook and poked at the bear who grunted and departed deciding he would not press his luck any further !

Sandford was looking for a map of Peterborough, but found there was none. So he surveyed the town and made one. Then he needed a lithographer to copy the map and on finding none locally he had to go to Toronto and buy the equipment to make copies of the maps himself. He surveyed and made maps for other towns like Cobourg, Newcastle and Toronto.

Eventually his popular maps attracted attention and he obtained a job as surveyor for one of the newly formed railway companies.

The rest of the Fleming family arrived in Canada in 1847. Sadly the business went bankrupt in Kirkcaldy. Brother Alexander remained in Kirkcaldy, eventually setting up again in the furniture trade. Sandford had arranged that his father would take over the local flour mill, the Humber Mill and Saw Mill, but the venture was not a success. Eventually with David, who had lost all his wood carving tools in a fire, they bought 400 acres of land. Here his parents lived out the rest of their lives at "Craigleith".

In 1849 Sandford went to Montreal to sit the exams for the "Dominion Lands Surveyor's" licence. This he duly obtained signed by the Governor Lord Elgin. While there he found himself in the company of an angry crowd pursuing the Governor Lord Elgin as they felt they had not been given adequate compensation for their losses over the rebellion of 1837. He soon found that it was not Lord Elgin who was so much the target as the Parliament building. The mob were out to destroy it and eventually set it on fire.

Fleming had been in the building while sitting his surveying exams and knew that the library was full of rare books. He rushed in to try to save the books but he was too late. However he did see a very large and heavy portrait of Queen Victoria and with help he removed it to safety as well as a gilded crown which was not reckoned to be much value, so he kept it in his home for many years until it mysteriously disappeared.

In 1849 when he was only 20, he founded the "Canadian Journal of Literature and History". In 1850 he co-founded the "Canadian Institute" and at one of the meetings only two people showed up. But Sandford was not prepared to give up. It eventually became the thriving 'Royal Canadian Institute'.

In 1851 he designed the first Canadian Postage Stamp which had a Beaver in the centre. He also had his design of the Peterborough Cemetery adopted that year. He had many talents and was a good artist. Some of his Scottish drawings were published in Canada, in a book of etchings also containing Canadian drawings. His Scottish contributions were St Peter's Episcopal Church, Parish Church and the new Burgh School, all in Kirkcaldy.

Canada's first postage stamp designed by Sandford

By 1852 he was surveying for the railways and David was also gaining an excellent reputation as a wood carver. In 1853 he was taken on as Chief Engineer in the building of the Canadian Northem Railway and in 1860 when the Prince of Wales was touring Canada and the railways, he assisted in showing him round.

In January 1854 he set out to visit Peterborough and found himself travelling with Jean Hall who was also making for her home in Peterborough after visiting Mrs Hutchison in Toronto. After the train journey they got into a horse-drawn sleigh to travel to Peterborough, when unfortunately there was an accident and the horses and passengers landed in a snowdrift with the sleigh a write-off. Sandford was knocked unconscious for a time and thought he had several broken ribs. With passers-by he was helped to reach the nearest house, that of a Scotsman and here he was nursed by Jean and the local Doctor for a week until he was well enough to continue with Jean to Peterborough. That was the start of their romance.

Plaque in War Memorial Gardens, Kirkcaldy

On March 21st 1854 he wrote and proposed marriage to Ann Jean Hall. On March 29th he received a reply of acceptance. Friendship had blossomed into love and they married on 5th January 1855, when Sandford was 28 and she was 24. Jean was very special and important to Sandford all through his life and the family was always very close. There were nine children, five daughters and four sons. Son Frank born November 1855, died 1918, worked very closely with his father. Jean, Maude and Jeannie died before reaching five. Sandford Hall, born 1856 died in 1947 aged 92, Mary was born 1859, Lily Frances in 1861 Walter in 1868 and Hugh Percy, the youngest, in 1871. Jean died at the age of 57 in 1888.

Shortly after this Sandford was approached by the Red River Company and asked to help build their railway. He spent 10 years with them after which time he had gained a great reputation as an expert and was the consultant for three railway companies.

He returned to England briefly in 1863 to try to get Government funding for this project, and in the back of his mind he always had the building of the Canadian Pacific Railroad from East to West.

In 1863 he advocated that the railway companies should join up and form a Trans Continental Railway of 2000 miles.

This job with the Red River Company in 1863 meant he would be far from home most of the time and so he built a house at Halifax overlooking the Harbour which was to become one of the family homes. In 1871 he had a battle to try to introduce steel bridges into the railway route instead of the traditional wooden bridges which were frequently going an fire. Eventually he won.

The Church remained at the centre of his life and in 1871 he wrote "A short service for Sunday" and in 1877 a "Short Sunday Service for Travellers". He kept up to the end his church involvements and published several theological papers.

In 1876 the whole family went on a visit to Britain starting with Ireland and the Giants' Causeway and then going on to the West of Scotland before reaching Kirkcaldy. Unfortunately their holiday was marred by bad weather. In 1897 Queen Victoria made Sandford a Companion of the Order of St Michael and St George, a Knight of the Realm.

Sandford returned to London and Europe in 1878. When in London he decided to call on Thomas Carlyle whom he had never met. He introduced himself as having been born in Kirkcaldy in the year when Edward Irving came to preach, on the day that the gallery collapsed in the Old Kirk. Thomas Carlyle and Edward Irving had, for a short time been teachers in Kirkcaldy. Edward and Thomas had been great friends, Edward had been in love with Jane Welsh whom Carlyle later married after Irving, unable to gain release from his betrothal to Reverend Martin's daughter, married her. The marriage soured him and all his energies went to his preaching. His little son also named Edward Irving died at the age of 14 months. In Carlyle's words "he went wrong in the end but he was a great and good man". Thomas's step brother John had lived and died in Canada. Both Thomas Carlyle and Sandford Fleming were acquainted with Provost Patrick Don Swan of Kirkcaldy. Thomas Carlyle was not really receiving anyone at that time, except old friends. However he agreed to see Fleming and when he took his leave, Carlyle shook him warmly by the hand and said how glad he was that he had come to see him.

Fleming went to the Paris Exhibition during 1878 and while there he was presented to HRH Edward Prince of Wales (Bertie) who invited him to join him at the Opera the next night. Sandford had many walks and talks with Edward after that.

At the end of his holiday in 1878 he was called back to finish the last part of the railway route, that which took the track through the Rocky Mountains. He had already surveyed an alternative route which had been ignored and now the Company was faced with problems it could not solve and so they called him back. The complete route of the east to west railroad track was finally joined up in 1880. Now, sadly passenger trains no longer traverse the complete route (freight only). However certain scenic sections like the Rockies are open during the summer months.

In 1880 he became Chancellor of Queens University Canada and later turned down the opportunity to become the Principal. In 1884 St Andrews University awarded him an Honorary Doctor of Law followed by Columbia in 1885 and two more Universities, Queens and New York.

In 1882 the Town Council of Kirkcaldy made him a Burgess and Freeman of the Burgh. In 1897 he was knighted "Knight of the Company of St Michael and St George" becoming Sir Sandford Fleming KCMG.

In 1912 he gave land in Halifax for building a Memorial, the 'Italian Tower' to commemorate 150 years of Nova Scotia. It stands within Fleming Park.

Sir Sandford wanted all the countries of the British Empire to be connected by the cable so that telephone and telegraph connections could be easily made.

Standard Time and International Time

Sandford was worried about the problem of time and distances on the railway. He persuaded Canada to introduce the 24 hour clock, cutting out am and pm in the timetables.

What had finally prompted this move was when visiting Ireland Sir Sandford arrived at the local station to catch a train at 5.30 in the afternoon. When no train arrived he asked the stationmaster why it was late. The stationmaster replied that Sir Sandford was 12 hours late as the train left at 5.30 in the morning !

Australian Pacific Cable

This was another of Sandford's dreams, started in 1879 and completed in 1902, 23 years after it had been first discussed. In 1893 Sir Sandford went to Australia and New Zealand with one of his daughters, via Honolulu, visiting also Italy and the pyramids in Egypt. The cable scheme was completed in 1902 and the telephone/telegraph link was established connecting Canada and Australia over thousands of miles.

Different countries had been involved in the construction, not all British. So in 1902 Sir Sandford worked for an "All Red Line" to join up all the Commonwealth countries around the world. Originally he wished Britain to allow him to 'acquire' the uninhabited island of Neka, belonging to the West Indies, but the British Prime Minister would not permit this. That is the island where Prince Margaret spent holidays at Mustique and where recently Branson's island holiday home was destroyed by fire.

War in 1914 prevented the 'All Red Line' from going ahead.

Plaques and Statues.

The Kirkcaldy Plaque was unveiled on September 21st 1973 by Provost John Kay, in the War Memorial gardens. It was organised by the Historic Buildings and Architectural Sites Board of Canada. A maple tree was planted behind the plaque.

"Inventor of Standard Time and Pioneer in World Communication, Fleming was born in Kirkcaldy and trained in engineering and surveying before emigrating to Canada and settling in Peterborough in 1845. He soon moved to Toronto but retained a lifelong interest in his birthplace which he visited frequently. In 1882 he was made a Burgess and Freeman of the Town. He was builder of the Intercolonial Railway and as chief engineer of the Canadian Pacific Railway conducted surveys of the transcontinental route. His proposal, presented to the

Canadian Institute in 1879, outlining a worldwide uniform system for reckoning time, and his advocacy of a cable route linking Canada with Australia, earned Fleming universal recognition. He was knighted in 1897".

Canadian Plaque. A similar plaque was unveiled in Peterborough on September 22nd 1973 by Mr John Fleming, Sir Sandford's great grandson.

Australian Plaque. A statue was erected in Australia on 15th May 1988 in memory of his pioneering the underwater cable route between Australia and North America.

In 1915 Sir Sandford died in his Halifax home and is buried in Ottawa.

References
"No Better Inheritance" *Jean Murray Cole* 1990
"Man of Steel" by   *Robert McNeil*
"Empire Builders" *Lawerance Burpee* 1915
"Born in Kirkcaldy" 1952 *D.C. Thomson*
"Famous Fifers" *Ronnie Wood,* Fife Regional Council 1977
"Fife Shopkeepers and Traders" 1820-*70 Campbell*
Kirkcaldy Plaque and Maple Tree, War Memorial Gardens.
Museum in Peterborough (Visit)